Kart Racing

Paul Challen

PowerKiDS
press

New York

Published in 2015 by **The Rosen Publishing Group, Inc.**
29 East 21st Street, New York, NY 10010

Library of Congress Cataloging-in-Publication-Data
Challen, Paul.
Kart racing / by Paul Challen.
p. cm. — (The checkered flag)
Includes index.
ISBN 978-1-4994-0172-1 (pbk.)
ISBN 978-1-4994-0133-2 (6-pack)
ISBN 978-1-4994-0163-9 (library binding)
1. Karting — Juvenile literature. I. Challen, Paul C. (Paul Clarence), 1967-. II. Title.
GV1029.5.C425 2015
796.7—d23

Developed and produced for Rosen by BlueAppleWorks Inc.
Art Director: T. J. Choleva
Managing Editor for BlueAppleWorks: Melissa McClellan
Designer: Joshua Avramson
Photo Research: Jane Reid
Editors: Joanne Randolph/Marcia Abramson

Special thanks to Flamboro Speedway, Collison Racing and Ciarra Collison

Photo Credits: cover Jaggat/Dreamstime; title page Nildo Scoop/Shutterstock; TOC, p. 8 top, 12 top TachePhoto/Shutter-stock; p. 4–5 Janetlee323/Shutterstock; p. 5 left Jaggat Rashidi/Shutterstock; p. 5 right Galina Barskaya/Shutterstock; p. 6 top Bundesarchiv, Bild 183-B1007-0016-001/Kohls, Ulrich / CC-BY-SA; p. 6–7 Nationaal Archief/Creative Commons; p. 7 right Cobra bubbles/Creative Commons; p. 8–9 Jaggat Rashidi/Shutterstock; p. 9 left Endurodon/Public Domain; p. 9 right, 18 top, 24 left Margo Harrison/Shutterstock; p. 10–11 Baloncici/Shutterstock; p. 10 top, 13 right, 14–15, 18–19, 18, 20 left, 25 right M. McClellan; p. 11 right, 16 Nildo Scoop/Shutterstock; p. 12 bottom Andy Rhodes/Dreamstime; p. 13 left Neacsu Razvan Chirnoaga/Dreamstime; p.14 top Ohmega1982/Dreamstime; p. 15 left, 25, 28–29 Neil Lockhart/Dream-stime; p. 15 right Terry Poche/Dreamstime; p. 16 top Claudio PlanetKart/Public Domain; p. 16 bottom; p. 17 Tony Leone; p. 19 right Brian Patterson Photos/Shutterstock; p. 22 D100a/Creative Commons; p. 23 Imago/Keystone Press; p. 24 top Nicky Rhodes/Shutterstock; p. 24 right Lawrence Weslowski Jr/Dreamstime; p. 26 Alexander Sandvoss/Dreamstime; p. 27 left Walter Arce/Dreamstime; p. 27 right Thesupermat/Creative Commons; p. 28 left Ddcoral/Dreamstime; p. 28 top Swisshippo/Dreamstime; p. 29 top Oskar SCHULER/Shutterstock

Manufactured in the United States of America

CPSIA Compliance Information: Batch #CW15PK: For Further Information contact: Rosen Publishing, New York, New York at 1-800-237-9932

Table of Contents

What Is Kart Racing?

Kart racing is a form of **open-wheel car racing**. That means that the car's wheels sit outside of its body, unlike a regular car that has its wheels covered by fenders.

Karts are much smaller than other cars that compete in races. The different levels of kart races are determined by how big a kart's engine is, and how old the driver is. Although you can start driving a kart around age five — and some people start even younger — the youngest age division for racing is for eight-year-olds.

Kart racing is a powerful, exciting sport and a great way to make new friends.

CIK-FIA

The organization that governs kart racing is the International Commission of Karting, or **CIK** (the French name is "Commission Internationale de Karting").
CIK is part of the International Automobile Federation, or FIA (French: Fédération Internationale de l'Automobile), which also governs Formula 1 and other international forms of car racing.

SAME FAMILY, DIFFERENT SPEEDS

It is common to see karts, often called go-karts, at amusement parks and fairs. But while go-karts usually have top speeds of about 15-20 miles per hour (24-32 km/h), the powerful engines in top-level go-karts allow them to reach speeds of up to 160 mph (257 km/h)!

If you go to an arrive-and-drive kart track, whether indoor or outdoor, your kart will not go as fast as a racing kart, but it will be faster than the amusement park variety.

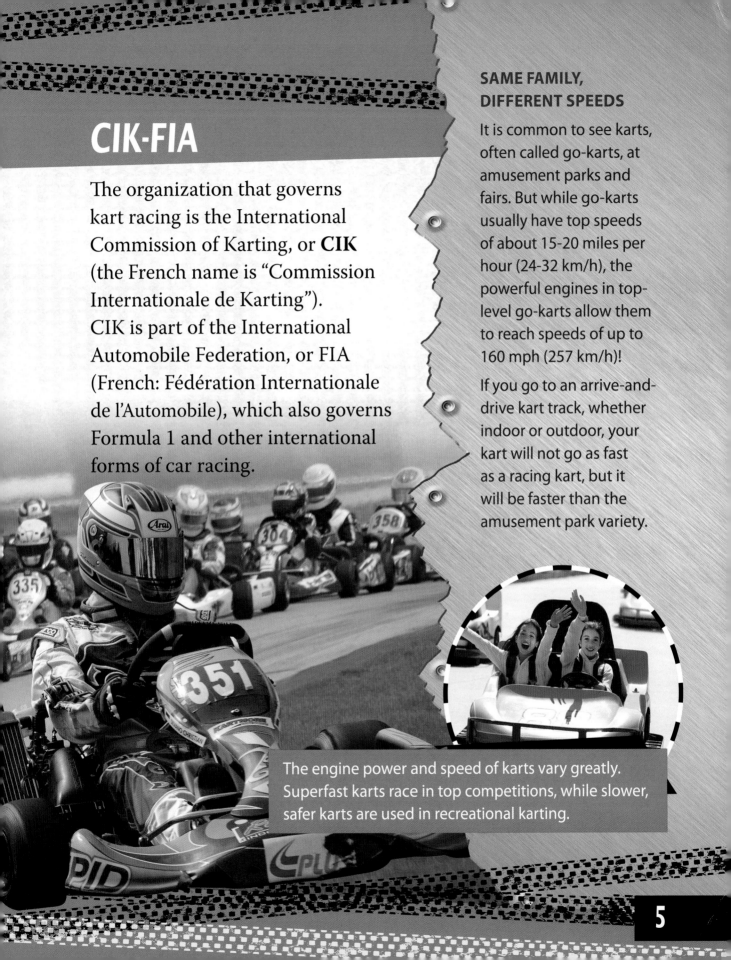

The engine power and speed of karts vary greatly. Superfast karts race in top competitions, while slower, safer karts are used in recreational karting.

The History of Kart Racing

A race car designer named Art Ingels built the first kart in 1956. He adapted the same ideas he was using to design much bigger cars to the smaller karts. The McCulloch company was the first large-scale builder of karts, producing their first in 1959.

Karting became popular in the United States, and soon its popularity spread to Europe and Australia. There are now karting races all over the world.

Karting rapidly spread around the world during the 1960s. It found a large following in Europe.

Karts were first produced for young drivers, but soon adults were also very active in kart racing.

Affordable Motorsport

One of the main reasons that karting has become so popular is that it is a very affordable form of auto racing, as opposed to other forms such as stock car and Formula 1 racing, which can be very expensive. Because it is relatively cheap to compete in, many racers start in karting before moving on to larger cars.

Kart racing is the safest and least expensive way to introduce drivers to motor racing.

The Kart Racing Formats

There are three main kinds of kart racing, determined by the size of the track, or circuit, the cars race on, or the overall length of the race. The three kinds are **sprint racing**, **road racing**, and **speedway racing**.

Sprint karts race on a paved course with left and right turns.

In sprint format races, karts race on circuits ranging from a quarter-mile (.4 km) to over one mile (1.6 km) long. In sprint racing, drivers usually compete in shorter races that qualify the highest finishers for a final, and some form of point scoring is used to declare an overall winner. These races are usually quite short, and the **Karting World Championship** is held as sprint races.

Speed and great passing skills are most important for drivers in sprint car racing.

Road Racing

Road racing events are held over much longer distances, sometimes taking as long as 24 hours to complete. In the United States, this form of racing is known as enduro racing. These races usually happen on longer road circuits, and drivers who are successful usually follow a more cautious, long-term strategy than in sprint racing.

Speedway races take place on tracks specially built for kart racing. These tracks are usually about a quarter-mile (.4 km) in length, and karts that race on them are specially built to handle lots of turns. In competition, qualifying races are usually held before the top drivers compete in the finals.

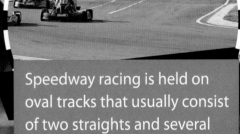

Enduro karts are very fast and are raced on big tracks such as Daytona International Speedway and Road America.

Speedway racing is held on oval tracks that usually consist of two straights and several left-turn corners.

9

The Kart

Kart engines are much smaller than those found in larger racing cars, but they can still be quite powerful. Some engines are standard production engines, while others are custom. Because of the way they work, these engines are known as four-stroke or two-stroke engines.

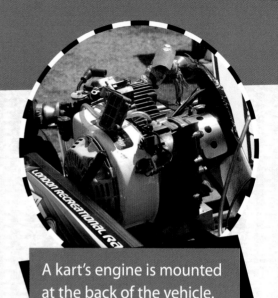

A kart's engine is mounted at the back of the vehicle.

A two-stroke engine will produce more horsepower than a four-stroke engine of the same size. Two-stroke engines are specially built for karting. They require more fuel and more maintenance. Four-stroke engines can be custom made for karts or they can be common utility engines. They are more fuel efficient, more reliable, and easier to maintain than two-stroke engines. Most beginners start with a four-stroke kart.

Not all karts are built the same way. The chassis of a kart is designed for specific races and recreational-type karting.

The Chassis

A kart's **chassis,** or "skeleton," is made of steel tubing. Most karts have an open chassis, which means there is no roll cage to protect the driver. Some karts have a caged chassis which does have a protective roll cage. The type of chassis depends on what type of track the kart races on, and what speeds it can attain.

The Tires

A kart driver and his or her team will choose tires that are best suited for the kind of racing conditions that they will be facing. Tires known as slicks are best for dry tracks, while rain tires are best for wet weather. In all cases, the tires used on karts are much smaller than those you would find on other forms of racing cars.

SUPERKART

Many people think of Superkart as the "Formula 1 of karting" because the karts used in this form of racing reach the fastest speeds of any karts – sometimes as fast as 170 mph (274km/h)! Superkarts have a longer chassis than other karts. They also have a semi-enclosed body and a rear wing. This gives Superkarts an aerodynamic look similar to that of F1 cars.

The CIK-FIA Superkart Championship is the fastest race of all kart races.

The Driver

Kart drivers must be physically fit, mentally alert and ready to adapt to any kind of weather conditions. Because the karts are fairly light, traveling at high speeds around corners requires great control. And to be successful in endurance races that may last many hours, drivers need to have a lot of stamina.

To race successfully, drivers have to do a lot more than simply drive as fast as they can. They need to take weather and track conditions into account, realizing that some parts of a race circuit can be more dangerous or tricky than others. As well, smart drivers will know the racing habits of their rivals, and be aware of how to take advantage of mistakes like sloppy cornering.

Kart racing drivers must adjust their driving tactics to different weather conditions.

Mastering the proper steering techniques is an important part of winning a race.

Protective Clothing

A competitive kart driver needs a lot of protective equipment. Different kinds of races have different rules about what a driver must wear, but the basics are the same.

A suit made of protective material is essential, and boots must be worn to protect the feet and ankles. Drivers also need racing gloves, and a full-face helmet is a must. To be safe, it is also a good idea to wear rib protection, and a brace to support the neck in back of the helmet.

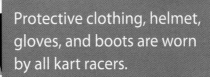

Protective clothing, helmet, gloves, and boots are worn by all kart racers.

The Tracks

There are four different types of tracks:

- sprint tracks
- dirt ovals
- road courses
- paved ovals

Sprint tracks are built to resemble small road courses, with right and left turns.

Sprint tracks are shorter paved tracks, designed for races that are also short in length.

A dirt track places demands on a kart that are quite different than those of a paved track, so karts that compete in **dirt races** must be built with special chassis and tires.

Paved oval tracks have asphalt surfaces. Ovals range from small racing rings to large quarter-mile (.4 km) tracks.

A road course is a circuit either specially built for racing, or a series of city streets adapted for racing. Unlike an oval track, these courses combine straightaways and left and right curves.

Finally the paved oval course is a longer circuit than a sprint track, but follows the same basic oval shape. Karts racing on this course complete a set number of laps in every race.

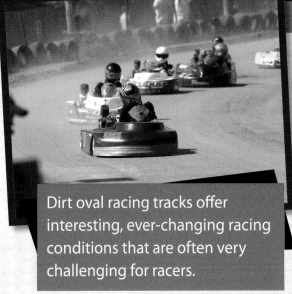

Dirt oval racing tracks offer interesting, ever-changing racing conditions that are often very challenging for racers.

Road circuits are outdoor circuits of more than 0.93 miles (1.5 km) in length. These tracks are shared for other car and bike racing sports.

⚠ FAST FACT

Karting takes place on indoor and outdoor tracks, but most serious races are held outdoors. It is also common for tracks to feature a combination of both, with most of the racing taking place in an indoor facility, with short stretches outdoors as well.

Racing Associations

Organized kart racing is governed by associations – that is, organizations that establish rules, plan series of races, and award prizes. Associations can be big and international, or small and local.

Karts are raced worldwide following the rules of CIK-FIA.

The Commission Internationale de Karting (CIK or CIK-FIA) was formed in 1962, and its headquarters are in Paris, France. The CIK holds the annual Karting World Championship, the most prestigious competition in karting. It takes place once a year, each year in a different country.

CIK-FIA also organizes yearly European Superkart Championships. Superkarts have aerodynamic bodies and race on car circuits that are at least 1.5 km (0.93 miles) long.

Karting in the United States

The **World Karting Association** is the group that governs karting in the United States. It was started in 1971, and has about 4,000 members in the United States and also Canada and Europe. Their mission statement says that the WKA's goal is to "provide a safe, fair, consistent, fun, and affordable environment for the beginner, hobbyist, and future stars of Motorsports to fulfill their racing dreams."

The **International Kart Federation** is a US-based organization that started in 1957 as the Go-Kart Club of America. Art Ingels, the "father of kart racing," was one of its first members. The IKF published its first rules for karting when it began, and has been doing so ever since. Its mission is to "foster strong and fair competition; to provide reasonable rules for the various types of competition; to administer the competition program with impartiality; and to reduce the hazards associated with this sport."

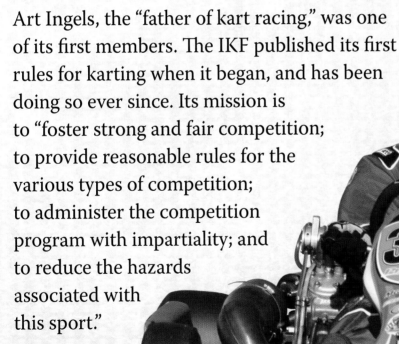

Kart races have a strong following in the United States.

Competition

Depending on the location, and what association governs karting there, it is possible to start kart racing as early as age five with "Kid Karts."

Junior competitive racing can begin at age eight, and takes place in age classes. In the United States, kart racing age classes are usually organized in three-year divisions, and when a driver reaches 15 or 16, he or she usually qualifies as a "senior" racer.

Young people make up a big part of any kart racing event, and on race day, it is usual for about half of all the drivers to be juniors.

Racing karts helps develop decision-making skills and quick reflexes.

Race day is a great event for drivers, their teams, and fans.

Get Licensed

To make sure everyone is safe and the races are run at a high standard of competition, associations that govern karting grant licenses to drivers, and prohibit unlicensed drivers from racing. There are many different types of licenses, depending on the driver's age and the type of racing they would like to do. But in general, to get a license, drivers must pay a fee and get the signature of their parent or guardian (if they are not adults). Beginning and young drivers also must practice for and pass a driving test and a written test.

WILL POWER

Australian-born Will Power started driving karts when he was just six years old. His dad, Bob Power, was an open-car racer. Will Power began racing in 1989, when he was eight, and never looked back. By age 15, he was racing cars on dirt tracks. Then he polished his racing skills on tough courses in Australia, Europe, and the United States. Since 2006, Will Power has been driving an IndyCar and living in North Carolina. He has racked up 21 IndyCar wins so far!

Indy driver Will Power began driving karts at age six.

The Race

Depending on the type of race and the association governing it, there are several rules all drivers must follow in karting. Just like in any sport, rules keep the competition fair and the competitors safe.

Rules cover a vast array of factors. Technical rules include how a kart's engines and body must be designed, while competitive rules include safety regulations, how many drivers can enter each race, and how points are awarded in a karting series. And just like in any sport, drivers and their teams are responsible for being aware of all the rules.

The officials announce the winner of a race by waving a checkered flag.

In any large-scale kart race, drivers compete in qualifying rounds to determine who will take part in the championship race on the "big day." This is similar to the format used in Formula 1, NASCAR, and other top-level racing.

The winning driver does a lap with the checkered flag.

Kart Racing Flags

Also similar to other forms of racing is the system of displaying **flags** in a kart race. When waved by race officials, these flags tell the drivers important information about weather and track conditions, and other things they need to know while driving.

Green Flag
The start of a race or all-clear track conditions.

Red Flag
The race has stopped. Drivers must pull off the track right away when safe to do so. This often happens when the weather has become too bad to race.

Yellow Flag
Warning, or caution. Often, this is because some kind of accident has occurred. When the yellow flag is up, drivers must slow down and cannot pass any other drivers.

Black Flag
You have been disqualified from the race! Drivers who have committed some breach of the rules will see this flag, usually along with their kart number.

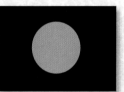

Black Flag with Orange Disk
Displayed with the driver's number, this means the driver's kart has a mechanical problem and the driver must pull over to get it fixed.

White Flag
The final lap of a race for the race leader.

Blue Flag
The driver is about to be overtaken by faster drivers and should yield to them.

Checkered Flag
The race has ended. If a driver sees this one first – he or she has won the race!

Championship Action

There are many top-level kart racing series – that is, a group of races in which drivers win points depending on how they perform, with the overall winner being the driver with the most points. Here are some of the most important series:

The Karting World Championship

Organized by the CIK, the Karting World Championship has taken place every year since 1964. Drivers from all over the world take part. The first world champion was Guido Sala of Italy, who won in 1964 and 1965. Most recently, Nyck de Vries of the Netherlands won in 2010 and 2011, with Flavio Camponeschi taking the championship in 2012, and Tom Joyner of Great Britain winning in 2013. Over its history, the Karting World Championship has changed the specifications of the kart's engines several times.

Revved-up engines belch smoke at the start of one of the Karting World Championship races.

The Manufacturers Cup Series

The World Karting Association's Manufacturers Cup Series for sprint racing is a six-race series that takes place at tracks in the United States and Canada. It begins with a December race at the famous Daytona International Speedway in Florida, and has grown to more than 600 drivers. There are four divisions: the "rookie" for drivers seven to 10 years old; a series of divisions for racers between 12 and 15; the "senior" category for drivers 15 and up; and "masters" for drivers over 35.

The WKA Road Race Championships

This series of road races, sponsored by the World Karting Association, takes place on courses usually used by larger racing cars. These large tracks allow karts to reach high speeds, and races are held in several categories all over the eastern United States.

MAX VERSTAPPEN

Dutch driver Max Verstappen was born in 1997. In 2013, he became the KZ1 (the highest class of kart racing) World Champion at only 15! Speed runs in Max's family — his father is a former F1 driver, and his mother was a successful kart racer. Both his grandfather and uncle are former top road racers as well!

Verstappen began karting when he was seven years old.

Crash Course

Experienced drivers know that there are risks that come with any kind of motor racing. But by following the rules kart racers have been able to maintain an excellent safety record.

Unlike many other types of racing cars, karts are not usually equipped with roll cages or seat belts. That means that drivers rely on their suit, helmet, and other safety equipment to protect them. It is important for all this equipment to be made from material that will protect a driver who can be thrown from the kart and slides along the ground.

Officials keep the racers safe by waving a yellow flag to have them slow down in case of trouble on a racetrack.

Medical personnel and ambulances stand ready at races to help if needed.

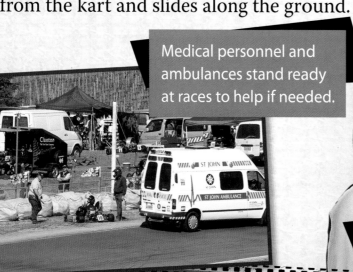

All motorsports are watched over for safety by officials, from karting to Formula 1.

The Officials

Most karting associations have rules stating that officials can inspect any kart and any driver's equipment at any time during a competition. These inspections include such things as helmets, racing suits, and other protective clothing, as well as the engine, brakes, and chassis. Officials can also check for fuel safety, and will make sure that nothing has been added to the fuel to give any kart an advantage.

CORNERING SECRETS

Experienced drivers spend a lot of time practicing their speed on corners. They try to come out of each turn quickly to pick up speed on the straightaway. And they avoid coming into the corner too quickly, as that means having to brake and slow down all through the turn.

Having proper cornering techniques can help a driver win races.

Run-off areas are spaces off the track put aside for vehicles to leave the track safely in case of emergency.

Stars Start in Karts

Although kart racing involves cars that are quite a bit smaller and slower than Formula 1 or other forms of racing, it is considered a great way to prepare for higher levels of motorsports. Because the basics of karting are more or less the same as any type of racing, karting offers a lower-cost way to get into the sport that is also safe and fun. Many top drivers got their start in karting, including some of history's greatest.

MICHAEL SCHUMACHER

German driver Michael Schumacher is the greatest Formula 1 racer of all time. He has won the F1 World Championship seven times, and has many individual records, such as most race victories in a career and most wins in a season, most world championships, and the fastest lap recorded in a race. Schumacher got his start in kart racing at the age of four, when his father built him a small kart, and won his first race at the age of six! By 1987, at the age of 18, he had won both the German and European kart championship, before moving on to bigger cars.

Michael Schumacher started racing karts at age four.

DANICA PATRICK

American Danica Patrick is considered the greatest woman auto racer of all time. She has had great success in open-wheel IndyCar racing, winning the 2008 Indy Japan 300 race. That win was the only one in the history of IndyCar racing by a woman. Patrick also came third in the 2009 Indy 500, the highest finish ever by a woman. She has also competed in NASCAR racing, and won the award for most popular NASCAR driver (male and female) in 2012. Patrick was born and grew up in Wisconsin, and it was there that she got her start in racing in 1992, as a kart driver at the age of 10.

Danica Patrick started her racing career at age 10 driving karts.

ALAIN PROST

French driver Alain Prost won four World Formula 1 championships in the 1980s and 90s. He also won 51 F1 Grand Prix races, a record until Michael Schumacher broke it in 2001. Prost played many sports as a kid, but got his start in auto racing when he discovered karting on a family vacation at age 14. In 1975, he won the French karting senior title, and moved to larger cars soon after.

Because of his intelligent approach to racing, Alain Prost was known as "The Professor" by racing fans.

You and Kart Racing

To get started in karting, the experts recommend visiting a local track and talking to people who have been racing for a while. They'll give you some tips on starting out. Next, try driving a kart at an indoor or outdoor track that offers rental karts. You don't need to bring any equipment; it will all be included. Just be ready to have a great time as you get a feel for the sport. You won't be able to become an F1 or NASCAR driver until you are older, but karting gives even very young people a chance to get started!

There are indoor kart tracks that can be a fun way to try out the sport.

Many outdoor kart tracks rent karts for casual drivers.

Driving Fun

Like any sport, kart racers get better with more and more practice. Also, experienced drivers can give you tips on how to improve both your performances and your safety. As has been the case with many top drivers, learning about karting can open the doors to getting into other forms of racing.

And no matter how you do competitively, karting can be a fun way to spend your spare time and meet friends. Happy racing!

Dutch racing driver Beitske Visser started with kart racing and worked her way up to GP3 Series.

Kart racing is a great competitive sport for kids that builds their motor skills, coordination, and self-esteem.

Glossary

chassis A kart's "skeleton" or inner frame.

CIK The Commission Internationale de Karting, the world governing body of karting.

dirt race Kart race that takes place on oval dirt tracks.

flag The banner used by race organizers to signal drivers. Each color of flag signals a different message to the drivers.

International Kart Federation An organization run by its members to provide rules and management for kart races.

Karting World Championship The most prestigious karting championship, held every year and organized by the CIK.

open-wheel car racing A form of auto racing featuring cars with wheels found outside the car's body.

speedway racing Kart races that take place on tracks specially built for auto racing.

sprint racing Short-track kart races.

road racing Kart races held over longer distances, often on road courses.

World Karting Association The group that governs karting in the United States.

For More Information

Further Reading

Dugan, Christine. *Final Lap! Go-Kart Racing.* Teacher Created Materials, 2012.

Norville, Alison G. *Kart Racers.* Enslow Publishers, 2010.

Randolph, Ryan P. *Karts.* Gareth Stevens Publishing, 2011.

Websites

Due to the changing nature of Internet links, PowerKids Press has developed an online list of websites related to the subject of this book. This site is updated regularly. Please use this link to access the list: **www.powerkidslinks.com/tcf/kart**

Index